ALSO BY SHIRLEY KAUFMAN

*The Floor Keeps Turning*

*Gold Country*

*Looking at Henry Moore's Elephant Skull Etchings in Jerusalem
    During the War*

*From One Life to Another*

*Claims*


TRANSLATIONS

*My Little Sister,* translated from the Hebrew of Abba Kovner

*A Canopy in the Desert,* translated from the Hebrew of Abba Kovner

*The Light of Lost Suns,* translated from the Hebrew of Amir Gilboa

*But What: Selected Poems of Judith Herzberg,* translated from the
    Dutch with the poet

# RIVERS
# of SALT

POETRY BY

*Shirley Kaufman*

---

COPPER CANYON PRESS / PORT TOWNSEND

PUBLICATION OF THIS BOOK IS SUPPORTED BY A GRANT FROM THE
NATIONAL ENDOWMENT FOR THE ARTS. ADDITIONAL SUPPORT TO
COPPER CANYON PRESS HAS BEEN PROVIDED BY THE ANDREW W.
MELLON FOUNDATION, THE LILA WALLACE-READER'S DIGEST FUND,
AND THE WASHINGTON STATE ARTS COMMISSION. COPPER CANYON IS
IN RESIDENCE WITH CENTRUM AT FORT WORDEN STATE PARK.

*Library of Congress Cataloging in-Publication Data*
Kaufman, Shirley.
    Rivers of salt : poetry / by Shirley Kaufman.
        p.        cm.
    ISBN 1-55659-055-5 : $11.00
    1. Jerusalem – Poetry.   2. Jews – Poetry.   I. Title.
PS3561.A862R58   1993
811'.54 – dc20   92-45859

COPPER CANYON PRESS
POST OFFICE BOX 271
PORT TOWNSEND, WASHINGTON 98368

Some of these poems, often in earlier versions, were first published in the following periodicals:

THE ATLANTIC: "The Core"

CALIFORNIA QUARTERLY: "By the Rivers," "Notes to my Daughters"

FIELD: "Meatballs," "A Japanese Fan," "At the Station," "Ganges," "Jealousy," "Longing for Prophets," "Peace March," "Lemon Sponge"

THE IOWA REVIEW: "Waiting"

IRONWOOD: "Milk" (Section 2, originally titled "Perfection")

LILITH: "Milk" (Section 1)

MĀNOA: "Riding the Elephant," "Forever After"

THE MASSACHUSETTS REVIEW: "Survival Kit"

THE NEW REPUBLIC: "The Status Quo"

OPEN PLACES: "Forty Years" (originally titled "Bellagio"), "Cineraria," "Driving Through Delhi"

PLOUGHSHARES: "The Temples of Khajuraho," "Bread and Water"

POET LORE: "Drifting"

POETRY: "Annunciation"

POETRY NORTHWEST: "On a Photograph of Myself as Grandmother"

THE SNAIL'S PACE REVIEW: "Four Entered the *Pardes*," "Wild Flowers" (originally titled "Gratitude")

SOUTHERN POETRY REVIEW: "Three Songs of Love and Plenitude"

TIKKUN: "Decisions" (originally titled *"Intifada"*), "The Wife of Moses" (originally titled "Zipporah")

THE THREEPENNY REVIEW: "Leftovers"

WESTERN HUMANITIES REVIEW: "Lake," " 'The World's Longest Tramway' at Albuquerque"

"The Status Quo," "Peace March," and "Decisions," originally published separately, have been gathered in this volume under the title *"Intifada."*

"Happy Endings" was first published in *A Celebration for Stanley Kunitz on his 80th Birthday,* © 1986 The Sheep Meadow Press, N.Y.

I wish to thank the Corporation of Yaddo, and the Rockefeller Foundation for inviting me to work at the Bellagio Study Center in Italy where a number of these poems were written.

This collection, now revised and enlarged, won the Alice Fay di Castagnola Award of the Poetry Society of America.

*for* BILL
*again, and always*

# CONTENTS

## One

## Two

## Three

## Four

WHO HAS TWISTED US AROUND LIKE THIS, SO THAT
NO MATTER WHAT WE DO, WE ARE IN THE POSTURE
OF SOMEONE GOING AWAY?

*Rainer Maria Rilke,* The Eighth Elegy


WHOEVER LEAVES HIS HOUSE
HAS ALREADY RETURNED.

*Jorge Luis Borges*

# ONE

## Waiting

After the fervor
of fists on the breast and fasting,
after the last plea slips through the heavenly gates
as they close and we've run out of things
to atone for, I want to start over.
The way my grandmother purified her heart
in the women's section.
But the rains are late, we're not forgiven,
and autumn won't come.
A few blurry showers in the north,
not in Jerusalem. No loosening.
No green rinsing of the trees.

We can't do anything
but wait. Fear sticks to our minds
like the black lice of newsprint.

The dead are so light, they don't wait,
don't have to consider what might happen.
The wind simply lifts them over.
Michael was edging off all summer,
week by week he grew lighter
until he left hardly anything behind.
A man grows small in the distance
as he unwillingly walks away, walks backwards
so we can see the little twist
of his smile. His face already taut as a mask
from which his breath trickled out.

Last week clouds came, a dark insensible mass
above the hills, but nothing fell. We wait
in front of an empty screen

when the movie is over and the next one hasn't begun.
Too dull or dazed to get out of our seats.
Someone is sweeping the refuse
in the aisles. Someone is torching
a car in the next block. Someone
is shooting into a gang of boys.
Someone is slashing open a woman with a knife.

Students at the vocational high school are printing
a book of poems. On celebration, they tell me.
Will you give us a poem?

We walked to his grave on the mountain
in a dry wind, our backs to the sun,
crossing an endless grid, hundreds
of empty plots evenly bordered with cement,
mingy homes for the homeless
waiting to be assigned.
"He will make peace . . . for us . . ."
When they finished the *Kaddish*
the men took turns and shoveled the soil back.

Autumn won't come, but the days are shorter
leaving us suddenly.
The heat never closes its eyes.
Staying up with the moths
and the souls of the lost ones
we're not really stranded. We just have to
lie here in the dark, soothed after love,
getting used to how it is.

There are black rubber masks in our closet.
When you tighten the buckles
and smooth the rubber snugly over your face
and attach the filter according to the printed instructions,

you can breathe fresh air
for about six hours. That's what they tell us.

Celebration. A poem. One of the birds
that woke me up today sang three notes
over and over. We stood on the balcony
watching them fly from the roof
and the eaves next door
in and out of the pines with their flawless wings.
It has to be one of the common birds,
you said, a bulbul or greenfinch.
It can't be a jay. They mostly screech.
Maybe a blackbird. Quick, on the branch.
Flicking its yellow beak,
it took off. One sunbird
dangled below us giving off sparks.
There were high-pitched calls
and a steady twitter. Most likely
it was a crested lark, you said,
but I can't tell you how any of them sing.


NOVEMBER, 1990

## Longing for Prophets

Not for their ice-pick eyes,
their weeping willow hair,
and their clenched fists beating at heaven.
Not for their warnings, predictions
of doom. But what they promised.
I don't care if their beards
are mildewed, and the ladders
are broken. Let them go on
picking the wormy fruit. Let the one
with the yoke around his neck
climb out of the cistern.
Let them come down from the heights
in their radiant despair
like the Sankei Juko dancers descending
on ropes, down from these hills
to the earth of their first existence.
Let them follow the track
we've cut on the sides of mountains
into the desert, and stumble again
through the great rift, littered
with bones and the walls of cities.
Let them sift through the ashes
with their burned hands. Let them
tell us what will come after.

## Four Entered the Pardes

Even the outer edge of paradise
was chancy for anyone still alive.
They might have drowned
in the quicksand of their minds
from fasting, splitting each word,
hearing the wheels of Ezekiel's chariot,
the racket of wings, already smelling
oranges on the celestial trees, splashing
through blossoms white as fire
around the letters on God's skin.

I could never say what I wanted
outside my body or where my soul was
if I had one, but reading into the night
I thought of it happening to me,
floating up through the seven circles
closer and closer to the last
unknowable heaven. No shadow to hide in,
every mean little trick exposed
just as I made it over the fence,
the terrible radiance finding me out.

*Do not say water when you reach*
*the stones of pure marble.* As if
there were syllables for the sound
of light. Only one survived.
Ben Abuyah turned heretic, ben Zoma
went mad, ben Azzai died. Akiba
hurled himself home. I groped
for my unlit body on the bed.
My eyes began to shuffle the dark,
to straighten the carpet.

## The Lowest Place on Earth

Tight little curls fleecing the hills
like the new growth on shorn lambs.
On the way down
it is green for awhile from the last rain,
the skin of the earth still tender.

I wish you would tell me we are not
driving through a deep moat, dark
palisades of stone, unscalable walls
above us and the crows circling
in their black coats.

The sky is slick as a sheet of plastic
over the Dead Sea. And we settle
our bodies on it, face up,
fixed in the unappeasable salt.
No matter how hard we pull each other down,
we discover we cannot sink.

# The Wife of Moses

*. . . The Lord met him, and sought to kill him. Then Zipporah took a sharp knife and cut off the foreskin of her son, and cast it at his feet . . .*

EXODUS 4:24, 25

Something went wrong
when he told her to pack
and went on listening
to voices she couldn't hear.

It wasn't her job,
this blood on her fingers,
this cut flesh, red love-bite
in the sand.

The desert widens between them
like an endless argument.
His mouth is too soft
for God's omnivorous rage,
fish will die, the river
stink and lice and flies
and boils and the rest.
Slice of the covenant: blood
on the doors.

He's off to his mountain.
She'll lose
what she saves,
fall out of the future
thankless, nothing to lean on
but her own arms,
holding the small face
unfathered anyway, crying
between her hands.

# The Core

It goes on burning in his brain
after the last war: standing
on guard in the desert at night
he'd watch a great blast of fire
he knew would destroy him. At sunset
the cliffs of Sinai open their veins.
The Red Sea closes over the chariots.
We think it will never end
all summer, his chain-smoking, jumpy
fingers during our visits in the ward.
There are redwoods in California
that feed for months on the heat
of their own destruction. You can see
where fires have guzzled their way
to the core, until the tree,
what's left of it, stands
gaping around its absence.

# Annunciation

You've got to believe, she says,
the child will be planted in me
Monday. She is becoming
heavy, she is holding a secret,
a pomegranate, in her fist.

When they took her away,
she wore sandalwood beads
around her head
like a belt over temptation.
It didn't help. A pigeon
is flapping at her perfect ear
and the Word is already
in her.

Each morning she sweeps the dust
into tiny nests. Memory
works like an electric fan scattering
everything, spells, cries
of the sybil she was
in her first life.
She wakes into trance.
Now she drinks sweet
death in a glass
and tells us she'll kill
herself next year. The match box
is ready for her bones.
She is a saint, but we know
better, resourceful as ever

we instruct her gravely in the uses
of language. *Like. Like.*
The stone is only a stone.
As if we never believed
our own lies. She knows
the angel has come.

We sit on the bench, feeling
our flesh sag into the space
between the slats, stirring
the gravel with our shoes,
wanting the small particulars,
the bird with the yellow throat
we wish we could name, to multiply
until there's no place for fear.

Not to sit stupid with failure,
watching the old woman who crawls
sideways along the path,
her head turned over her shoulder
always in terror seeing
who follows her. Not
the man marching with his fly
unbuttoned or the girl
who swings like a scared spider
over the grass beyond reason,
but this bench. The dark patch
under it. The hospital garden.
Bare trees silver against
the wall and the crisp weeds,
the late sun, her face
with the flicker of a face we know.

We fasten our jackets as the wind
gathers the last leaves
from a branch and burns them,

a heat from which nothing comes.
She thinks we are pretending
not to be worried. She thinks
we are lost. We are
permitted to visit the garden
to let her amuse us. After
an hour we have to go.

# Lemon Sponge

Once I lived in a house
that trapped the sun.
The walls were smooth adobe.
I could hear the clay breathe
through little straw beaks.
At night my body stayed warm
with what it remembered.

\*

What lets us be who we most are?
Suppose we only had to know
the climate, what grows where,
how rich or shallow the soil is.
A kind of field guide
for dislocated souls:
how to be rooted, how to be
born in an ancient cycle
from seed to seed,
dust of our old selves settling
over a new season.

\*

Sometimes I hear the siren
for the first time and the air
doesn't shiver, only my bare legs
running across the field, the dry
summer grass and the dusty thistles.
That was three wars ago.
I drove down to Jericho
to find you during the cease-fire.
I baked your favorite cake,
the lemon sponge, and we sat for awhile
together next to your gun.

\*

You have to get used to fear,
not fear exactly, but a long unease.
To walk it off in the streets
and supermarket. You have to
get used to God,
wrote Elsa Lasker-Schüler,
as if he were food
one cultivates a taste for.

\*

There are days when I feel like
an infant's rattle. A little
shake. A little smile.
Not yet, we keep saying
as if time were benevolent.
Last night I dreamed
we were speeding in a car,
too far from home
to know where home was.
I had tied the frayed ends
of my seat belt in a double knot.
Wasn't that strange? And the sky
fading, white-hot at noon,
powdery as plaster. It wasn't the dream
that upset me, but your face
when I told you, troubled and distant,
not asking what happened next.

# Intifada

## 1 THE STATUS QUO

The sand is still hot in September
everyone drives to the beach and we float
in our light bodies watching the red ball
roll to the bottom of the sky and the sea
darken and the waves lift us
willingly toward the shore as if
nothing has happened we can go back
to the same life never mind that it's gone
like a road in the desert after a flash flood
like the houses we blew up yesterday

## 2  PEACE MARCH

In Benares I saw corpses
carried high in saffron robes
to the sacred fires. We carry
these photographs as offerings
to the night. Not like the blind
who walk forever with their arms out.
Not like the holy men smeared with ashes
on the way to the temples.
But like a family, too long on the road,
who by their lassitude
have let this happen.

We walk silent through the streets,
some holding torches, others
dark blow-ups of all the slain children.
Small mouths of disbelief,
how stunned they are
in the young faces.

> *Second Anniversary*
> DECEMBER, 1989

## 3  DECISIONS

This morning after her second cup of coffee, finishing
the front page, she decides the future no longer
matters. What a relief. And the past too. Always
stepping into the next ruin, balancing on the next
ledge, making it crumble again. Ancient eroded
vineyards in the Judean hills. She can forget
what happened, all that pile-up of memory and guilt
like accidents on the bridge when the cars smash
into each other behind the first collision. We don't
have to hold our necks, she thinks with a sweet release,
or assess the damage or take notes from the other driver.
It doesn't matter it doesn't. She keeps the news
to herself like a secret drinker, not able to give it up.
The boy with his leg blown off. The dutiful children.
What she is in her own eyes, the bulk of her fear.
Yesterday she had to decide between chocolate-orange
and mocha-pecan. The best ice cream in Tel Aviv
they told her. Decide. Decide. As if her life
were the life she'd chosen. As if anyone's life

# Survival Kit

6:30 a.m. The Early Risers
Aerobics Class
at the Jerusalem YMCA.
*Good Morning Sunshine* and rhythmical others
all the way to the final stretch
and Satchmo growling
*What a Wonderful World.* Oh yes
stepping out to the street
where invisible men sweep the garbage.

\*

Blue fistfuls of plumbago
burst over the fence. Bunches
of hot pink blossoms from the oleanders
drop on our heads. Hibiscus
with their incendiary tongues.
Spikes of lavender. Fire-eating
cactus in the rockery.
Excessive as we are, still having
everything to lose.

\*

Our friend remembers how Helen Keller
pressed her fingers against his throat
to hear him recite the Sabbath prayers.
Hebrew is such an undulating
language, she said.
And the prayers for the dead?

\*

Shula's children have something
in their hair. Draw me a picture,

I want to know the size.
It's a life-size picture,
a spot as big as the center of my watch
from which the hands go around.
I can't see the legs. Are there legs?
Then another dot, smaller, a baby.
New generations every day.
So small you can't find them.
Do they jump? No, they crawl,
one head to another.
They live on blood.

\*

We know a man who went to jail
so he wouldn't have to shoot a child.
What wouldn't I do?

\*

When John Lennon was killed
we huddled together, a few
expatriates talking about the old highs
and the new graffiti, about songs
that come back when you need them.

Gaby put on the record
and we got very quiet, drinking
black coffee at midnight
and listening hard to the music.

Then into the snow that swept down
suddenly from Syria, walking fast
as it stung our eyes and melted,
taking the short cut home.

\*

Was Ruth so lonely in a strange land,
gathering only what was left
of the corn, afraid
she would always be alien?

*

There are seven thousand pelicans
in the Hula nature reserve. Huge flocks
in the Beit She'an valley
feasting on fish in the fish ponds.
Three tons a day. They dropped in
on their way to Africa
and they won't leave.
Men fire in the air
to scare them off
but they won't be scared.

# Hamsin *Breaking after Five Days*

For you also, your desk at the window
in the next room, the tip of the cypress
turns like a green wrist

lifting the long tree after it.
Something flutters the ivy on the walls
across the street, blue

widens between the two pines.
Sudden. Out of the ache and heaviness.
The simmering heat.

Once in Sarnath we saw those unwinged
beings over the Buddha's head
fly upward, weightless.

We thought that the world could change
like the wind's direction. The clean sweep
of falling in love.

Blessed be whatever sprinkles
a little water on the dust
to make it settle.

# By the Rivers

That spring he was fourteen,
sun on the walls, stale air
sweet in Bergen-Belsen for the first time,
he told me he thought of the nurse
who held him when he was small.
He found a corner
where they did not catch him:
rush of the brilliance and the heat
and no one there. He opened his clothes,
hunched over his wasted body,
and made it spill.

\*

The poem wants to look forward, not
back, but out there as far as it can see
are ruins: body of Abel body of god body
of smoke. And no recognizable
child to mourn.

So it begins with longing.
Or with fear, that old dog
stinking beside it, scabby and blind.

And all the time the future
is pushing up uncalled for
under the cold ground, or gliding down
like the first snow, wet syllables
that melt and soak up the darkness.

The poem wants to get out of
where it is. But is instructed
to remember. In shameless daylight.
By the rivers of salt.

## Bread and Water

After the Leningrad trials, after solitary confinement
most of eleven years in a Siberian Gulag, he told us
this story. One slice of sour black bread a day.
He trimmed off the crust and saved it for the last
since it was the best part. Crunchy, even a little sweet.
Then he crumbled the slice into tiny pieces. And ate
them, one crumb at a time. So they lasted all day. Not
the cup of hot water. First he warmed his hands around it.
Then he rubbed the cup up and down his chest to warm his
body. And drank it fast. Why, we asked him, why not
like the bread? Sometimes, he said, there was more hot
water in the jug the guard wheeled around to the prisoners.
Sometimes a guard would ladle a second cup. It helped
to believe in such kindness.

## Snow in Jerusalem

After it stops the air is still
whirling around our house and the pine trees
shake out their iced wings the way
dogs shed the sea from their bodies
after a swim, a white crust slides
like shingles down the backs of the branches,
soft clumps loosen themselves from
sills and ledges, fall past our window
with the swoosh of small birds
or of moths at night that beat themselves
senseless against the lamp until
we switch it off and reach for each other,
warm and slightly unraveled under
the worn nap, under the flannel
of the snow sky, under the overhanging
sorrow of the city listening to the
plop, plop, it's all coming clean now,
starting to thaw a little from the inside.

# TWO

## Notes to my Daughters

You were the reason for staying.
It's always the children who leave,
not the mother. It was the end
of winter, isn't that always
the best time. Freesias suddenly
out of the mud, little milk teeth,
plum trees unbuttoned and the sky
on the Bayshore freeway to the airport
lined with blue tile.

Do you feel abandoned,
now you are women?

\*

From the ridge of our mountain
we can see the Judean wilderness
slide to the bottom of the world.

Sometimes the parched air ripples
with dust as if everyone's beating
carpets and the shudder of wind
is like nervous laughter out of the caves.

It's all getting smaller and farther.
The earth wears a thin green fuzz
where the sheep graze
stubby in the distance as if
they were cut out and pasted there.

\*

I've learned what he knows,
how to tell sonic booms from the others.
To mean what we say.

First thing in the morning
in the Valley of the Cross
when the night is still drying
on the leaves and the red poppies
stand up straight
as if pulled by strings,

a man balances on his head
in the wet grass, we're behind
two Ethiopian joggers
and a woman walking her boxer.

The rest of it empty
like the future no one plans for.

\*

There's an overwrought smell of jasmine,
tiny wax flowers, wiry stems
around the railing of our balcony.
Too tame to fly, the vines
catch on and keep climbing.

Scent of my old life, where the light
falls back of my shoulders
into your day.

\*

If not for the three of you, if not
for the two of us,
if not for my cousin's strawberry jam
at breakfast and a woodpecker
attacking our jacaranda
outside the kitchen window, drilling

so loud we don't hear
the seven o'clock news, if not
for persimmons and the first
green oranges we wait for
and the small hard peaches
that arrive in the market in April,
if not for the ripening
when we expect it, bulbs
of new garlic spread out to dry
just when the old garlic's rotting,
if not for Mary's latest recipes,
meat loaf with carrots and cumin
and fennel soup, and Mussa's
bottles of green-gold oil
from his olive trees in Beit Safafa,
and the crested larks, little tan females
singing their hearts out on both sides
of the green line, if not for
the bulbul's five purple eggs,
and all the glad birds on Yom Kippur
praising the parked cars
in the empty streets and the prayers
of the ones who keep praying,
if not for the archaeologist unlocking
the safe in the museum to show us
the yellowed bone, the rusty nail
still hammered through the heel,
if not for the gilded dome and the silver dome
balloons and bells
and the muezzin calling, peace
marches around the Old City wall and me
on the ramparts following my body,
if not for the two of us, waves
of white surf breaking
over the hawthorne's arthritic limbs,

if not for what flickers as joy
in the middle of grieving,
what could I say when you ask me
whether I'm happy.

\*

One day I'll look up at the hills
and they won't be there. Lately
I think about my death.
It keeps me connected to the world.

I wonder if you'll come
to put little stones on me
the way Jews do to keep the unliving
where they belong.

\*

I wish I could learn how
to strike matches in the wind
so they won't go out in my cupped hand.
I wish I could peel an orange
in one long ribbon that doesn't break.
I wish you were with me
in this hard land waiting for the first rain
after a long dry season
when the sky tilts and spills over
making a fresh start,
stirring the dust into muddy trickles,
clearing everything but not
washing it away.

## A Japanese Fan

When I hold a chicken over the gas
to singe the blunt ends of feathers
sticking from legs and wings, the random
hairs, the loose flap dangling
over the broken neck, fat
crackles and the bumps in the skin
burn black. I pluck the singed hairs
one by one. It takes me an hour
to clean two chickens.

This morning at the bus stop on Jaffa Road
a woman was fanning herself with a paper fan.
A cherry tree and a tiny snow-covered
Mt. Fuji were painted on it.
The sun was so hot we could barely
breathe. I watched her climb slowly
up the mountain. The air got lighter.
When she wriggled her toes in her sandals
she could feel the snow.
She wiped some of it on her cheek.

I need a Japanese fan in my kitchen.
I need a little wind to get me
from place to place.
When I tell you about the snow
my words are small origami birds
with the meanings inside.
I want you to unfold them
and look at them under the light.

The wings of this chicken
have sharp little elbows.
I have to unfold them

and flatten them over the flame.
I think of my father with his words blocked,
regarding his hands. How he was trying
to lift them, the weight
of his waxy fingers, trying
to remember what to do.
When I held his dead hand in my hand
he seemed to be holding me.

The blue flame hisses when the fat melts
and jumps into orange. One tip
of a red-hot finger over Mt. Fuji.

# Yahrzeit

All day regret and appeasement flicker
in the memorial flame, long-burning candle
I light on the Hebrew date
when I remember, as variable
as the world is variable
for its wandering Jews.

I see him like a peddlar
under his sack, sandman, huckster,
itinerant lover returned
from the cold plot next to my mother,
some shabby motel-room Willy Loman,
to sell us what?

I wish I could find him
in the small flame, startled
and happy, reeling his catch in,
playing the big ones.
Whatever he knew about loss
he never told me.

When he was his own boss,
and his workers went on strike,
I called him the dirtiest word I knew:
*Capitalist.* I shouted and wept:
*You filthy capitalist!* We tried
to forgive each other.

There is so little to go back to.
Now that I'm edging toward the place

where everything happens
for the last time,
I need to hold him
in this cupful of light.

# *Milk*

You pump it from the six goats
morning and evening
and renew your own. The baby
is harnessed to your back,
her dark head wobbling. Your life
and its order that isn't mine.

I've come as close to you
as I can. Over the sudsy milk
I watch your hands,
the little tough spots
at the tips of your fingers.
We tell it again:

how grandma stopped eating
and spit out her mush,
how the rice fields were burning,
how you stayed in your room
with the candles and incense
and played your guitar.

Once in our terrible anger
you struck at me wildly
and I couldn't see. Light
was a bolt from the laser
riveting my eye. Black flakes
floated between us for a long time.

The buckets are full. I lift
your daughter from her warm pouch
into your arms

as if I were lifting you
out of my empty body.
We're not who we are

to our mothers. Even now
in this sweet flesh
isn't there something starting
to withdraw? The child
is reminded of herself.
She wakes to cry.


2


One goat has an udder the size
of a cow's. The weight of that
huge sack slung beneath her
seems to be more than she can bear.
She struggles to stay on her feet,
and you tell me she's overbred.
Some misplaced passion for cheese
or being the best.

I warm the goat milk on your stove
and think of how scared you were
to go to school for the first time,
how you wept in my arms
because you didn't know how to read.
You thought you must know already
what you would have to learn.
The way we cry till we're red at birth
not knowing how to live.

So we perfect ourselves, wanting
to come out grander than we are,
two women trying once more
like Piranesi after fifteen years

etching his prisons again
to get them right. The great beams
are stronger than ever,
shadows are denser than before,
the space in the front left corner
that seemed to be empty
is filled with chains.

Only to see more clearly
what is there.
We stoke the Rayburn with new wood
and carry the pots of milk
out to the shed.
There is a smell of goat cheese ripening.

## Leftovers

Men came to the door
when I was a child
and we gave them leftovers
on the back porch. Dolorous
lessons in poverty and caution.
The forms of hunger.
Deadweight of a body passed out
on the sidewalk. Nights
when my father didn't come home.
My mother brought them hot coffee,
but never asked them in.

*

What sins did she ever, working
the heels of her hands
through the silence of flour.
Unto the next generation:
her melancholy kitchen,
the smell of turnips, lamb shanks
boiling on the stove. Peel
the potatoes for tomorrow's stew.
Roll out the dough and the flour
rises like her soft sighs
into my rocking palms.

*

Because of the broken neck
of her first love
who fell off a horse in Poland,
and because of her marriage
to barley soup and the Depression,
and because of her amputated breasts,

and because she sang
"I'm Forever Blowing Bubbles"
until she was diapered and tied
in a wheelchair,

\*

before I could enter
the bone-china tea cups
of her memory and the Bug River
of her lost future, before
I could be her daughter,
she turned me into her mother.
Taught me the names of love
in her language: grief
and sorrow, sorrow and grief.
Translating with her shoulders
the forms of hunger.

\*

In Kiefer's painting
*Every Human Being Stands Beneath*
*His Own Dome of Heaven,*
rows of unplanted furrows fall off
the soft edge of the horizon
blank as the end of the world.
A tiny survivor sealed
in a glass bubble raises one arm
with no one to wave to.
A tent of pure oxygen seems
to be keeping her alive.

\*

Applesauce, everything mashed
and pureed, I fed her slack body
one spoon at a time.
And then she was gone,

a house boarded up behind us.
Men sitting on the steps
in their worn clothes, eating
our last night's dinner, cold
meatloaf on white bread.
The door was open
but the screen was latched.

# Lake

She is more lost to me than ever
where I stand on her birthday in the June light
next to a lake she never heard of.
The trees at the edge are dissolving
under themselves. She's not in my dreams,
she has returned to her first language,
drifting over the mountains
while my father rows the small boat.
His sleeves are rolled up
and he's milder than I remember,
though his suspenders are cutting his shoulders
and the oars blister his soft palms.
The mountains are upside down. They've left me
with someone on the shore.
I watch how she leans back
trailing one hand in the water,
her pinned hair starting to fall down
and her eyes crinkled. I forget everything
I had to tell her. If only she'd wave
before we are gone. If only I knew
what she's saying about the future
that makes her happy.

## At the Station

My aunts who sit side by side
in their wheelchairs at the Seattle Home
for the Aged never wanted to be aged
in Seattle. Never wanted to be always
together, last of the sisters
and nobody left to blame.

They behave like ex-lovers, bitter
but civil when they meet in a room
full of old friends who know better.
They are not certain who we are
or why they have to go
with us to America.

Marion is strapped to her chair
and plucks at the binding around her waist.
Fan begs her to stop. Little bird bones,
they are so brittle, shrunk back almost
to what they were in the beginning.
The trunks are already in the cart.

We are trying to make them smile.
We put small squares of chocolate
between their fingers and swallow hard.
They drink the sweet milk of reproach
and the sour milk of gratitude.
It runs down their chins.

Their eyes are wide open, looking
at someone behind the mirror.

He clicks his heels. He is Polish,
with a riding crop. He's at the station
where they left him in 1912,
waiting to kiss their hands.

# On a Photograph of Myself as Grandmother

FOR SAMIA AND SARAH

It's not a pose. They are so innocently
perfect against my arms,
though slightly unfocused.

I see myself sitting on the bench
between them in the sun
like someone I wanted to be.

I'm not ready. We are over-exposed,
our lips much paler
than they are,

the two girls already dissolving
in the hard light
that bleaches their hair

and drains the last color out of mine.
I am holding a book
wiped clean in the false radiance,

no print where my hand lies white
on the white page
and the children can't read yet

but they mouth all the words by heart.
I tell them again
how the lost bird looks for its mother,

an absence they almost
believe in, caught
in the middle of the book

where nothing is certain, listening gravely
to the sound a bird makes
when it's abandoned.

# "The World's Longest Tramway" at Albuquerque

Once on the Görnergrat I thought the wind
would sweep me out of my body,
all that immensity of light
and the gates wide open.
If I didn't look back
I'd be lost.

Looking back is the problem.
Every chunk of the poor earth keeps us
accountable, this scrub
and the dwindling pines
with their little white shelves,
one hill sliced flat,
and after that to the north
stubble, the parceled land, Los Alamos
on which the snow swirls
soft and elegiac.

# THREE

# The Temples of Khajuraho

At the airport waiting for our plane,
we sat next to a Chinese man.
He took off his shoe and sock
and massaged his foot,
working his thumb and fingers
over the sole and delicate arch
of the instep. Then he held
his whole foot between his palms
and forgave it, rocking it
gently back and forth.
His hands seemed to know
what his foot wanted.

\*

This woman pulls a thorn
from her heel and this woman
wrings water from her shampooed hair
and this woman paints her eyelids
in front of a mirror and this one
fastens bells around her ankle
and this one slips off
her transparent chemise
and this one smiles
at her dexterous lover
guiding him in.
An inexhaustible cheerfulness.

\*

And sweetly convivial,
so many figures
touching and stroking
the length of their bodies,

stone warming into flesh. They repeat
and repeat each other, pleasure
runs through his fingers
to her breast and back again,
a circular comfort, the curl
at the ends of their mouths
like the tenderness after.
Even their toes curl.

\*

Touts, cripples, blind
children who pluck at our sleeves,
all the dark versions of desire
are locked out behind the fence.
Twice a day we walk to the temples
while they run after us,
past a small lake, more like a puddle
of muddy water, three battered rowboats
tied up in the reeds. And a large
sign printed in English: *FLOAT*
>               *on the beauty of twilight*
>               *and twinkling of stars.*

\*

If we imagine hunger sometimes
it's not in our guts.
It's art we've come for,
art and the witty gods in the temples
promising bliss. We study
their postures of unresisting
grace. Your hand
slides over my shoulder.
In the half light
as in anything half seen,
the body remembers
what it wants to.

# Riding the Elephant

That's me up there on the elephant
smiling
with my mouth closed,
clutching the bar
that has just been fastened
across the box I'm caged in.

The ground seems farther
than it should be. The beggars
can't reach us.

The elephant lifts one wrinkled leg
and puts it down
and I think I'll tip over.
When there's no danger I invent it
the way I invent India.

The path is steep
all the way to the palace.
I let myself be happy a little,
squinting into the sun,
even hanging on tight. As if
I am still on my father's back,
hugging his neck,
his slippery shoulders
as he rides me to bed.

The palace is crumbling,
incandescent and pink
as the fevers of childhood,

green parrots flapping
through the trees, glittery dust
on the broken tiles.

I want to be dazzled. I want
to be lifted into the room
where mirrors tremble on every surface
when a match is struck,
to look at myself on the ceiling
tinseled with light, my body
rippling in the crazed glass.

It's the same body. The same awful bulk
I sit on in the grainy air.
I just have to hold on steady
while the long sinews of the mind weave
leisurely, like a trunk
that scoops up everything.

## Forever After

There's a wedding cake palace
in Akbar's ghost town.
Five tiers with a tiny cupola on top.
Each layer perfectly preserved.
Except for the sugary figures
of the bride and groom.
They're packed in a box
in the closet I left behind.

Humpbacked bony cows step over
their own dung, lie down
in the middle of the road
like aging odalisques
with heavy eyelids. Ugly
but hopeful. They make no excuses.

When the snake charmer
blows on his flute, the cobra
raises a dazed head,
unblinking, till the lid comes down
on the basket. It's there
in the dark, coiled.
And the difficult eyes
of the women behind their veils.

A man drops pale lumps of dough
in a boiling vat. When they turn gold
he lifts them dripping with oil.
They taste like dumplings I almost

remember. My tongue mulls them over.
Everything new is like nothing else.
I swallow them hot. Time
is a pond, they say here,
where the ripples will disappear.

## Driving Through Delhi

Everywhere her hands
or cut-off hands, brown skin
stretched over skinny wrists
that clasp our coins. Pinching
the stumps together.

She won't stop pressing
against closed windows
when the taxi slows down
or stops at a red light,
each time

she is waiting,
lifting her baby
wrapped in rags,
burned rims of her eyes
behind the glass.

As in my own dreams
when I'm abandoned, screaming,
and no sound comes out.
Hammering
at the whole deaf world.

The way she comes back,
scratching the windshield,
the driver telling us
not to, telling us
don't look,

revving the engine
while she stands there
not getting smaller
in the distance
as we drive away.

# Cineraria

I sit in his Delhi garden
drinking beer before lunch.
"You start with one toe
and let it get heavy."
He tells me he learned to relax
each muscle and let the pain go.
I lived in San Francisco
in the sixties so I'm right
at home. His porch is lined
with pots of purple cineraria.
Little imperialist flowers
from my own back yard.
Once he went to visit
Ginsberg and Orlovsky
in Benares. He wanted
to talk about poetry,
but they kept asking him
about the Ganges. "Peter
served tea like a Hindu wife."
Not exactly, I'm thinking.
Whatever we're sharing only
seems the same. Parvati
comes out of the kitchen
with ten arms and an extra eye.
If I wore her viridian sari,
if I had a tiny diamond
on the side of my nose, I still
wouldn't know about the next life
or the transmigration of souls.

# Ganges

In the dark there's no other side.
Only the river where every morning
the faithful prepare for death.
Small wicks flicker in the leaves
they carry and scatter a little radiance
on their faces, their thin shawls.

Cripples are wheeled into place
on wooden platforms, and women
squat in a line on the stairs
with tin bowls. The eyes of their babies
are dull already and soft
as water in a cupped hand.
Softer than ashes.
Vague as my mother's
when they finally closed.

What is it keeps us
nurturing the first loss
with our regrets and unspeakable pity,
wanting to step over the edge
if we can come back
forgiven? What is it
in the sickrooms?

The ones who enter the river
lift the dark to their mouths.
When they loosen their saris
their arms shine. All
the wet skin of the grieved world
bobbing and rising.

                    How simple
the frail light is on the white shirt
of the boy we follow, led
from one boat to another
until the last one
where he unties the rope
and shoves off. And how calm
when the river takes it
and sets it down on its gray back
letting it ride there, a light
so still it scarcely seems to be
breathing. Like the light
as the fever came down
when I wrapped her all night
in wet towels, soaking and wringing
until the breath was there
in her mouth again.
It's the past I look into,
but the past keeps growing.

The boy pulls hard
on the long oars, and our boat
nudges up to the ghat
where the dead are burning.
They are shoveling the ashes
from the last one into the water.

We row with smoke in our throats
through the smoke of morning.
It's already the next life.
The sun's on the rim of the old world
like the tip of a thumb.
We turn toward the shore.
The widows are wrapping their heads
in white, unwrapping

their floating shoulders.
Men stand in the river slapping
laundry on the black stones.

I hear the thwack.
And the chants of praise
getting louder. And the click
of rice striking tin
in the hands of beggars, the little
pale grains collecting.

# FOUR

## Wild Flowers

After everything I've forgotten, now
on the other side of the world I hid in
as a child, it's the same sun
running down my back, the same tick
of insects in the moist air.
When I stare into the tiny radiant pupil
of this blue-violet one and you say
*eye of the madonna*—the whole field
stares back in a golden nimbus,
leaves shine and the sweet quattrocento
faces I never prayed to.
There are daisies bunched in the grass,
red poppies, all the old flowers
I sang to, made chains from,
or sucked the milk out of,
shaggy and tender and on the verge.
And I'm down on my knees in the clover
where nothing has changed
or slipped through our fingers, still
looking for luck.

# *Three Songs of Love and Plenitude*

## 1 FETTUCINE

There's a white cloud rising from Alfredo's head.
A perfect fit. He is making pasta
on white marble, brushing it gently
on both sides with white flour.

The door is open to the kitchen garden,
and Angela is picking gray-green bristles
of thyme, rosemary with its tiny spikes,
tarragon and parsley. On this sunny morning

we are tender as fettucini.
If I caught that lizard in my hand
it would sing about happiness
if it knew how to sing.

## 2   TO KNOW

Gönül says there is a special word
for *know* in Turkish which stands
for visual experience. To keep it
separate from the rest of knowing.

In Hebrew there are two words
with three meanings. Carnal,
as used in the Bible, and the others.
You have to be careful.

Now when you sit on the edge
of our bed, I know the smooth muscles
of your back in more than one language,
but I touch you just to be sure.

### 3 ON THE TERRACE

We are eating newly picked pears
with Gorgonzola. The sun
and the fruit in our mouths,
the blue veins crumbling.

All night it rained and now the earth
is buzzing again in its warm crust.
Light skitters on the lake
like tiny needles getting rid of pain.

We are not waiting for anything
to happen. We are not going
anywhere, sitting here ripening:
Gorgonzola and pears.

## Happy Endings

I want to write stories with happy endings.
I want to write about the good life.
Even if it's somebody else's. Pliny
had a good life here in his villa.
Better than any life in Rome.
Terraces and porticos, a small hippodrome
for riding, hot and cold baths, gravel paths
between boxwood all the way
to Bellagio. And best of all,
one room remote and quiet
where he lay in the dark each morning
composing his thoughts.

There's a spider next to Pliny's
left knee, composing his web.
Pliny's nose is broken.
He sits in his carved robes
holding a book in his hand with one finger
missing, watching the lake.
He can barely see the view
from his little stone eyes,
the scrub and the honeysuckle have grown wild
on the cliff before him.

The spider is doing what he knows best.
He spins from the knee to the hand of the statue
as if he were swinging on a kite string
across the whole sky. The late summer air
is thick with insects. It's a good life.
Even if it's somebody else's.

# Jealousy

He is sulking again because whatever she does
it's the wrong thing or she's talking to somebody else
and he can't stand it. But he won't tell her about it
oh no he walks away from the museum shop and she can't
find him and even up in the galleries it starts, she
wants to tell him about the Botticelli in room number nine
and he is already ahead in number eleven. And out
in the street the others are drinking capuccino at a table
on the sidewalk and they have their arms around each other
lightly and she has to ask of they've seen him and there
he is dragging his feet in the distance, studying the windows,
spending the rest of the day attached to somebody else.
And she runs after him and asks why did you leave me,
and he says he wanted to look at Bergamo or Inverness or
Jaipur and she was too busy buying postcards, and that
isn't it at all, that's never it. And what can she do
but eat lamb's testicles or crawl on her belly
through the long night or fall in the lake
with her clothes on or throw herself from the parapet.
Until he is sorry and she is sorry and they are both
sorry until the next time which is in Santorini.

# Forty Years

for H.M.D.

Blue floats at the level of our eyes
as if the lake climbed out of itself
and up the mountains. As if
time were a lake we're in the middle of
treading water.
We notice the shine of the air,
the way the sunflowers lift
their burned faces to it.
The way the lizards race in and out
between the stones, providing.
The fervor of spiders.
Every day on the gravel paths
we brush their webs from our skin.

Cannelloni on the terrace
in the dazzling sun. Angela says
if we look at the mountain
on the left in the distance
we'll see the profile of a man.
We do. See the nose and the chin?
Like Mussolini. Yes. Wedged
into the view with his dogged jaw,
the unmistakable panzer face.

Forty years since you bivouacked
homesick across the lake
and they strung him up by his ankles
in Milan. Everything's new

when we get to the place
where you think your tent was.
The grass is paved over.
You're not even sure about the café
or what you are looking for,
or what you did with the picture
you bought for five cigarettes
of his dangling body.

BELLAGIO-LENNO

## Meatballs

After dinner we talk about nuclear war,
holes in the ozone. Small cups
of coffee. Earnest and passionate.

At six in the morning, the lights
of the village are like the last cinders.
The sky and the lake are one black hole
in which the rain keeps falling.

I stand at the window and count
my fears. They come so fast
I can barely name them. I barely
have time to feel their weight.
There are nine, ten, no twelve fears
before I get to nuclear war.
I can't do a thing about any of them.

All day I watch the rain's thin
curtain as the sky and the lake
turn gray again. I count
my fears. I make them the size
of small meatballs. I put them
on toothpicks. What else
can you do with fears?

By evening there are more meatballs
than lights in the village. And after
dinner we're at it again. Over
the coffee. Earnest and passionate.

At six in the morning, the lights shine,
the sky is black, the lake is black,
and the rain is still raining. I stand
at the window. I count the lights.

# *Drifting*

I saw the hand of Rasputin
cast in bronze and used as an oversized
paperweight on someone's desk.
The authentic hand. Smooth as Italian leather.
It was molded from plaster before he was killed.
Bought at an auction in Europe.
She was a collector.
She knew the value of everything.

I wouldn't like Rasputin's hand
on my desk, even though it wore the skin
over its fine bones like a soft glove
and healed the tsarevitch.
I wouldn't like her Samurai sword.
I'm glad I don't know what I'm worth.

There are days when the whole world
feels like somebody else's collection.
Even your hands. We walk
in another country and the mist
slowly rises above the lake
like all the heaviness we left,
dissolving.
Only it's not our heaviness.

\*

Sometimes, waking, I forget
where I am. The things around me
go on with their old existence
like props in a play, as if the curtain

has just risen on a room in an Italian villa.
It's not my play.

In the old life there was a photo
of Valentino on my desk.
Agnes Ayers was swooning in his arms,
the Sheik in a rapture of lips
without any words.

Benevolent uncles spoke in a language
I didn't know, their fleshy hands,
their anxious eyes smiling
as they patted me gently on the head.
Like watching a silent movie,
when they opened their mouths
like fish under water
I turned off the sound.

All that sweet absence.

*

Once I learned the thirteen principles
of Rabbi Salanter, but I remember
only seven: truth, diligence, honor,
repose, cleanliness, frugality,
and silence. If I collected words
they would have to belong,
like moss or fleas. Things you say
that I can believe in.

Honor reminds me too much of the Samurai.
I like repose. It belongs to this landscape
where even the lizards rest
when we stand still
and look at the wall together.

Naming the things of this world
you begin to own them.
Cyclamen. Mustard.
I can't manage so many flowers.
But I already know the word for lake in Italian.

*

Gulls wheel over Lago di Como
at sundown on their way south
trying to catch the last warm currents.
Their wings are white, then silver, and then smoke
when the light abandons them
and dusk settles in their feathers.

If you don't collect things,
it's easier to move. Easier to stand
on this cliff for another minute
and watch the leaves fall, one by one,
yellow, into the lake.
They belong to the air
for the time they are drifting.
It's a long way down.

PARDES  [page 7] Persian word from which *paradise* is derived, meaning "orchard" in modern Hebrew. It is generally agreed that to enter the *pardes* is a metaphor for the mystical (and dangerous) ascent of living souls. According to the Babylonian Talmud (*Hagigah* 14b), the four sages named in this poem entered such a metaphorical *pardes*. "Do not say water . . ." is a translation of the words of Rabbi Akiba quoted in the Talmudic text.

INTIFADA  [page 16] Arabic word for the uprising in the West Bank and Gaza strip by Palestinians protesting the Israeli occupation. It began in December, 1987 with young boys throwing rocks and with commercial strikes, and it became increasingly violent.

HAMSIN  [page 22] A hot, dry desert wind which fills the air with dust and makes it difficult to breathe.

YAHRZEIT  [page 35] Yiddish word for the anniversary of the death of a close relative, observed by lighting a candle and reciting the Kaddish.

Shirley Kaufman grew up in Seattle, Washington, lived in San Francisco for many years, and now makes her home in Jerusalem. Her previous books include *The Floor Keeps Turning*, which won the United States Award of the International Poetry Forum in Pittsburgh, *Gold Country*, *From One Life to Another*, and *Claims*. She has published several volumes of translations of Hebrew poetry and most recently collaborated with Judith Herzberg on the translation of her poems from the Dutch, *But What: Selected Poems*, which won a Columbia University translation prize. Among her honors are a fellowship from the National Endowment of the Arts, the 1989 Alice Fay Di Castagnola award for a work-in-progress and the 1991 Shelley Memorial Award from the Poetry Society of America.